AUSTRALIAN COOKING FROM DOWN UNDER

70 AMAZINGLY DELICIOUS AUSTRALIAN COOKING RECIPES FROM THE OUTBACK AND BEYOND

By Victoria Love

Table of Contents

Top 70 Australian Breakfast, Main Dish, One Dish, Appetizer, Salad, Soups, Stews And Dessert Meals

Australian Breakfast Meals

Australian Main Dish Meals

Australian Appetizer Meals

Australian One Dish Meals

Australian Dessert Meals

Australian Soups and Stews

Australian Salad Meals

Australian Breakfast Meals

Onion, Garlic and Basil Frittata

Ingredients

- 1 tablespoon oil
- 6 medium onions, sliced
- 1 teaspoon brown sugar
- 4 garlic cloves, roughly chopped
- 8 eggs, beaten
- 3/4 cup milk
- 1/4 cup leggo's pesto sauce, Traditional Basil
- 3/4 cup grated tasty cheese or 1/4 cup feta and 1/2 cup grated tasty cheese
- Salt, to taste
- Fresh ground black pepper, to taste

Directions

1. Take pesto, milk and beat them with eggs in bowl.

2. Cook the onion sprinkled with sugar in oil in skillet over moderately high temperature setting for ¼ hour, mixing from time to time or till onion become golden brown in color.

3. Add in garlic in the final FIVE min.

4. Take egg mixture and pour this onto onions in skillet and cook over moderate temperature setting for FIVE min.

5. Use the grated cheese as sprinkle all over egg mixture.

6. Add salt as well as pepper according to your own choice.

7. Cook the frittata under grill till set.

8. Transfer to a dish.

Nana Muffins

Ingredients

- 4 ripe mashed bananas
- 2 tablespoons sweetened condensed milk
- 1/2 teaspoon cinnamon
- 1/8 teaspoon nutmeg
- 1/4 cup brown sugar
- 2 teaspoons baking powder
- 1/4 teaspoon salt
- 2 cups flour
- Sugar

Directions

1. Mix everything together.

2. Scoop a heaping spoonful's into muffin tins which are coated with cooking spray.

3. Use little bit of sugar as sprinkle all over each one.

4. Bake for approximately 1/3 hour at THREE FIFTY (35o) degrees Fahrenheit or till muffins start to get brown in color over the top.

5. You can serve this delicious and exotic recipe with butter.

Potato Egg Casserole a La Hot Potato Salad

Ingredients

- 6 potatoes, peeled and diced
- 4 -6 hard-boiled eggs, peeled and chopped
- 3 green onions, finely chopped
- 1 tablespoon parsley, chopped
- 1 -2 teaspoon mustard
- Fresh ground black pepper
- 250 g low-fat sour cream
- 4 slices bacon, chopped and cooked
- 1/4 cup milk (optional)
- 1/2 cup cheddar cheese, grated

Directions

1. First of all, cook the potatoes in boiling water till soft.

2. Drain well and allow to cool.

3. Take potatoes, eggs and mix with spring onions, parsley and bacon in casserole dish.

4. Take mustard, sour cream and mix with black pepper and blend through potato mixture.

5. Bake, covered, for approximately 1/3 hour at ONE EIGHTY (180) degrees Fahrenheit.

6. Use the cheese as sprinkle.

7. Grill till become golden in color.

Prosciutto Breakfast Bake

Ingredients

- 20 g prosciutto
- 1 large egg
- 2 teaspoons red capsicums, diced
- 2 teaspoons red onions, diced (optional)
- Cracked pepper

Directions

1. First of all, trim the additional fat from prosciutto and layer into sprayed ramekin dish with fat in the bottom and second egg at the side.

2. Take egg and crack into dish.

3. Use the pepper and diced capsicum for topping.

4. After this, fold the prosciutto all over.

5. Bake for approximately ¼ hour at THREE FIFTY (350) degrees.

6. You can serve this delicious recipe over toast slice.

Chai & Raisin Oatmeal (Porridge)

Ingredients

- 1/3 cup quick oats
- 1 tablespoon chai tea mix
- 1/4 cup raisins
- 1/2-2/3 cup milk

Directions

1. Mix everything together.
2. Cook for 90 seconds in microwave, mixing for 60 seconds.

Mushroom Hotcakes/Pancakes

Ingredients

- 2 tablespoons olive oil
- 300 g Swiss brown mushrooms
- 2 cups plain flour
- 2 tablespoons baking powder
- 1 pinch salt
- 1 1/3 cups buttermilk
- 2 eggs (lightly beaten)
- 2 tablespoons chopped chives

Directions

1. Sauté the mushrooms in tbsp. of olive oil in sauté pan over moderately high temperature for TEN min, mixing from time to time till mushrooms become soft and all of the liquid has been vaporized.

2. Shift to a dish which is lined with paper towel.

3. Put aside

4. After this, wipe the pan neat and clean.

5. Take baking powder and sift with flour and salt in bowl.

6. Take buttermilk and whisk with eggs in jug till mixed.

7. Take buttermilk mixture and whisk into dry items till mixed.

8. Blend in mushrooms.

9. Blend in chives.

10. Use the oil for brushing the sauté pan over moderate temperature.

11. Spoon approximately TWO tbsp. mixture into sauté pan for each hotcake and cook for 120 seconds till bubbling.

12. Flip the hotcakes and cook for next 120 seconds or till become golden in color.

13. Delicious recipe is ready.

Pikelets Aussie Silver Dollar Pancakes

Ingredients

- 1 cup self-rising flour
- 1/4 teaspoon salt
- 1/4 teaspoon baking soda
- 2 tablespoons vanilla sugar, regular would work
- 1/2 cup milk
- 1 teaspoon vinegar
- 1 egg
- 2 tablespoons butter, melted
- 4 tablespoons butter
- 1/4 cup strawberry jam

Directions

1. First of all, sift the dry stuff together.
2. Take vinegar and put in milk and add in two tablespoons of butter.
3. Take egg and add to milk and blend it.
4. Take wet and add this to dry.
5. Then heat the griddle with melted butter.
6. Spoon a tbsp. of batter onto hot sauté pan.
7. Repeat the same process.
8. Turn over when bubbly.
9. You can serve this delicious and exotic recipe with jam over.

Baked Bean Scrolls

Ingredients

- 220 g baked beans in tomato sauce
- 1/3 cup grated tasty cheese
- 2 -4 slices mild salami, diced
- 2 spring onions, finely chopped
- 2 cups self-rising flour
- 30 g butter, softened
- 3/4-1 cup milk
- Extra milk, for glazing

Directions

1. Take the baked beans, cheese and mix with spring onions and salami. And put aside.

2. Sift flour in bowl.

3. After this, rub the butter into flour till mixture look like fine bread crumbs.

4. Form a well in the middle and pour in milk.

5. Then blend well to make a soft and tender dough.

6. After this, turn it onto floured surface and knead till dough become smooth.

7. Roll the dough into rectangular shape.

8. After this, spoon over bean mixture.

9. Roll up in order to enclose the bean mixture and chop into TWELVE scrolls.

10. Put them on oven tray that has been lined.

11. Use additional milk for lining.

12. Bake for ¼ hour or till golden in color.

Baked Eggs with Chive and Feta

Ingredients

- 8 eggs
- 1/4 cup chives, minced
- 2 green onions, minced
- 1/2 cup cream
- 1 teaspoon salt
- 1 teaspoon pepper
- 1/2 cup feta cheese
- 8 slices whole wheat bread, toasted cut in fingers that's in 4 long slices used for dipping in egg

Directions

1. Use cooking oil for coating the muffin tins.

2. After this, break eggs into EIGHT cups.

3. Take chives and mix with green onions into cream.

4. Add the salt and pepper to eggs.

5. Take cream mixture and pour this over eggs.

6. Use the feta cheese as sprinkle.

7. Bake for TEN min at FOUR HUNDRED (400) degrees Fahrenheit till eggs are done.

Egg & Bacon Muffin

Ingredients

- 4 English muffins, split
- 4 slices shortcut bacon
- 4 large free range eggs
- 4 slices Swiss cheese
- 2 tablespoons butter
- 4 teaspoons tomato relish
- Olive oil flavored cooking spray

Directions

1. Use the olive oil for coating the skillet.
2. Add in bacon. Then add in eggs.
3. Cook to your preference, turning the bacon one time.
4. Toast the muffins and spread the butter over.
5. Layer cheese and then layer egg on one half of every muffin.
6. Use the relish for topping.
7. Then top with 2nd half of muffin.

Australian Main Dish Meals

Chicken Breast Filled With Bacon & Cheese

Ingredients

- 1 skinless chicken breast
- 2 slices bacon
- 2 slices of matured tasty cheese
- 1 egg
- Breadcrumbs
- Dried rosemary
- Thyme
- 2 tablespoons olive oil

Directions

1. Fry the bacon and put aside.
2. Horizontally chop the chicken breast for making a pocket.
3. Put cheese and bacon in this pocket.
4. Beat egg in bowl.
5. Put breadcrumbs in bowl.
6. Add in thyme. Add in rosemary.
7. Take chicken and dip in egg and then dip in breadcrumb mix and put in skillet in oil over moderate temperature setting.
8. Cook till golden in color.
9. You can serve this delicious recipe with veggies.

Feta, Sweet Potato and Spinach Crustless Quiche

Ingredients

- 2 teaspoons olive oil
- 1 red onion, cut into thin wedges
- 1 garlic clove, chopped
- 600 g sweet potatoes, peeled and cut into 1.5 cm cubes
- 2 1/2 cups baby spinach leaves, I used 150grams
- 1 cup milk
- 6 eggs
- 200 g feta cheese, crumbled, can use low-fat feta if desired
- 1/2 teaspoon nutmeg
- Fresh ground black pepper
- 1/4 cup grated parmesan cheese
- 2 tablespoons pine nuts (optional)

Directions

1. First of all, coat the flan dish with cooking spray.

2. Cook the garlic and onion in olive oil in skillet.

3. Add in sweet potato.

4. Cook over moderate temperature setting, mixing from time to time till golden brown in color.

5. Add in spinach. Cook, mixing for 60 seconds till spinach wilts. Allow to cool.

6. Add in feta cheese.

7. Blend and put into prepared flan dish.

8. Take six eggs and beat them in jug with milk, pepper and nutmeg and pour this over veggies in the flan dish.

9. Use the parmesan cheese and pine nuts as sprinkles.

10. Bake at ONE HUNDRED EIGHTY (180) degrees Celsius for FORTY min or till become golden in color and puffed.

11. Let it rest for TEN min.

12. Then chop into wedges.

13. You can serve this tasty recipe a salad.

Chow Mein for Tomoko

Ingredients

- 2 tablespoons oil
- 1 medium onion, diced
- 500 g lean ground beef
- 1/2 large cabbage, finely sliced
- 3 celery ribs, finely sliced
- 2 medium carrots, cut into matchstick sized pieces
- 250 g frozen green beans
- 2 (40 g) packets chicken noodle soup
- 2 1/2 cups water
- 2 teaspoons curry powder
- 2 tablespoons tomato sauce (ketchup)
- 2 tablespoons soy sauce

Directions

1. Sauté the onion in oil in saucepan over moderate temperature setting.

2. Add in meat and sauté till meat changes its color.

3. Add in rest of items and blend well.

4. Heat to boiling.

5. Allow to simmer for ½ hour or till veggies are cooked, mixing from time to time.

6. You can serve this delicious recipe over the steamed rice.

Aussie Eastern-Styled Potatoes

Ingredients

- 6 potatoes, peeled and cubed
- 1 onion, chopped
- 2 garlic cloves, crushed
- 1/2 cup black olives
- 1 -2 tablespoon olive oil
- 1 tablespoon cumin powder
- 1 pinch salt
- 1 pinch pepper

Directions

1. First of all, cook the potatoes in oil in sauté pan over moderate temperature setting till ready and done.

2. Add in onions.

3. Add in garlic.

4. Add in cumin.

5. Keep on cooking till potatoes are cooked and onions become tender.

6. Then add in olives and keep on cooking till warm.

7. Add the salt and pepper according to your own choice.

Hoisin Chicken Kebabs

Ingredients

- 500 g boneless skinless chicken breasts
- 1/4 cup hoisin sauce
- 1 tablespoon fresh ginger, minced
- 1 tablespoon sesame oil
- 1 tablespoon rice vinegar
- 1 tablespoon sesame seeds (optional)

Directions

1. First of all, chop the chicken breast into pieces.
2. Blend the hoisin sauce, ginger, rice vinegar and sesame oil in bowl.
3. Preserve two tbsp. sauce to base the chicken.
4. Mix in chicken.
5. Keep in refrigerator, covered, for ¼ hour.
6. After this, thread the chicken onto skewers.
7. Cook the chicken on grill.
8. While cooking, base chicken with preserve sauce and turn from time to time till charred slightly.
9. Use sesame seeds as sprinkle.

Caramelized Steak

Ingredients

- 1 kg steak fillet
- 2 tablespoons soy sauce
- 2 teaspoons garlic, crushed
- 2 teaspoons mustard
- 1 orange, juice and zest of
- 2 tablespoons palm sugar, grated

Directions

1. Blend the marinade items in bowl besides steak.

2. Use half of the marinade for brushing the both sides of steak and put in covered refrigerator.

3. Then put the rest of marinate in refrigerator.

4. After this, cook the steak in butter in pan according to your own choice, turning and basting with the rest of marinade a couple of time.

5. You can serve this delicious recipe with veggies and mashed potatoes.

Mustard Lamb Chops

Ingredients

- 1/3 cup dry breadcrumbs
- 2 garlic cloves, crushed
- 1/2 teaspoon thyme
- 1/4 teaspoon pepper
- 1/4 cup Dijon mustard
- 4 shoulder lamb chops, trim off excess fat, slash the edges

Directions

1. Take crumbs, thyme and mix with pepper and garlic.
2. Blend in three tablespoons mustard.
3. Use the rest of mustard for brushing the chops.
4. Broil for FIVE min.
5. Then flip over and spread the crumb mixture all over chops.
6. Broil for THREE min or till preferred doneness is achieved and topping become golden brown in color.

Australian Style Hamburger

Ingredients

- 125 g beef, mince
- 1 egg
- 2 bacon, rashers
- 1 slice cheese
- 1 large slice onion
- 1 large slice Tomato
- 1 large slice beetroot (beets)
- 1 pineapple ring
- 1 hamburger roll
- Lettuce
- Margarine & tomato sauce (ketchup)

Directions

1. First of all, chop hamburger and roll in half and butter both of the halves.

2. Then toast both bun halves.

3. Sauté meat patty, onion and bacon rashers.

4. Turn over the meat and add the cheese over.

5. Sauté egg.

6. After this, butter bun and add in tomato sauce according to your own choice.

7. After this, assemble the hamburger.

8. Use the bacon, cheese and egg for topping.

Swordfish on Warm Avocado Corn Salad

Ingredients

- 4 swordfish steaks, about 150g each
- 1 shallot, chopped
- 2 ears corn, corn from 2 cobs
- 1/2 red bell pepper, finely diced
- 1 large Avocado, diced
- 1/4 cup chopped fresh coriander
- 1/4 cup white wine
- 2 tablespoons lemon juice
- 2 tablespoons red wine vinegar
- 1 tablespoon olive oil

Directions

1. First of all, sear swordfish in oil in pan for TWO min or till beginning to tender.

2. Take out of pan.

3. Use foil for covering.

4. Take shallot, red pepper, corn and add them to pan.

5. Cook, mixing, for TWO min or till beginning to get tender.

6. Add in avocado. Add in coriander. Add in white wine.

7. Steam, covered, for 60 seconds till heat through.

8. Take avocado corn mixture and put this over dishes and use the swordfish as topping.

9. Take lemon, vinegar and add to pan.

10. After this, whisk into pan juices.

11. After this, pour over fish.

Cheesy Spaghetti with Bacon and Peas

Ingredients

- 500 g spaghetti
- 1 cup frozen peas
- 1 tablespoon olive oil
- 1 onion, diced
- 4 slices bacon, cut into strips
- 2 garlic cloves, finely chopped
- 250 g smooth ricotta cheese
- 300 ml light cream
- 1 cup parmesan cheese, grated
- Plus extra parmesan cheese, to serve
- 2 tablespoons flat leaf parsley, chopped

Directions

1. First of all, prepare/cook spaghetti in pot of salted and boiling water as instructed on the package.
2. Take peas and add to pasta in final TW min of cooking.
3. Drain well and bring back to pot.
4. Sauté the onion in oil in sauté pan over moderate temperature setting till tender.
5. Add bacon and cook, mixing till begin to get crunchy.
6. Add in garlic and cook, mixing for ½ min.
7. Then drain off some fat.
8. Take ricotta, cream and add to mixture and blend over low temperature till combined together and heated through.
9. Take away from heat and add to pasta. Also add parsley and grated parmesan.
10. Toss well and add the seasoning.
11. You can serve this delicious recipe with ground black pepper and additional shaved parmesan.

Australian Appetizer Meals
Sausage Rolls

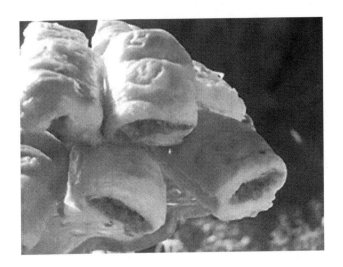

Ingredients

- 400 g ground sausage
- 300 g ground chicken
- 1 onion, finely chopped
- 3 garlic cloves, finely chopped
- 1 medium carrot, grated
- 1 medium zucchini, grated
- 1 cup fresh breadcrumb
- 3 tablespoons chopped parsley
- 1/2 teaspoon ground nutmeg
- Salt, to taste

- Fresh ground pepper, to taste
- 2 eggs
- 3 frozen puff pastry sheets, semi-thawed
- 1 tablespoon sesame seeds
- Tomato sauce, to serve

Directions:

1. First of all, use baking paper for lining the two baking trays.
2. Take both of the minces, garlic, carrot, onion, and blend them with seasoning, nutmeg, parsley, breadcrumbs and zucchini.
3. After this, beat in an egg in minced mixture and distribute into SIX same parts.
4. Chop the pastry sheets in half. After this, roll mince part.
5. Beat rest of egg.
6. Use the egg for brushing the pastry corners.
7. After this, roll up pastry for enclosing the filling and chop into SIX pieces.
8. Then put these sausage rolls on greased baking trays while the seam side down.
9. Use the egg for brushing.
10. Use the sesame seeds as sprinkle.
11. Bake for 1/3 hour.
12. Then reduce the temperature to ONE EIGHTY (18o) degrees Celsius and cook for TEN min or till become golden in color.
13. You can serve this delicious recipe with tomato sauce.

Healthy Chicken and Vegetable Sausage Rolls

Ingredients

- 1 cup fresh whole wheat breadcrumbs
- 500 g chicken breasts, minced
- 1 egg, lightly beaten egg
- 1 extra lightly beaten egg
- Salt, to taste
- 1 zucchini, finely grated
- 1 carrot, finely grated
- 1/2 onion, grated
- 1/4 cup chopped coriander leaves
- 1/4 cup chopped flat leaf parsley

- 4 sheets frozen puff pastry
- 1 tablespoon sesame seeds
- Tomatoes or sweet chili sauce, to serve

Directions:

1. Mix the unbeaten egg, chicken and crumbs in blender. Then put in bowl and blend well with herbs and veggies.
2. Then add the seasoning.
3. Put one pastry sheet on floured surface and halve.
4. After this, spoon 1/8 mixture long-ways along the middle of every piece.
5. Fold one corner of pastry over and tuck in.
6. After this, fold over other side for making roll.
7. Do the same with the rest of pastry and filling.
8. Chop the rolls into pieces.
9. Chop two small size incisions into every roll.
10. Put these rolls onto baking sheets.
11. Allow to chill for ½ hour.
12. Use the beaten egg for brushing.
13. Use the sesame seeds as sprinkle.
14. Bake till the rolls become light brown in color and are cooked through.
15. You can serve this delicious recipe with sauce.

Eggplant (Auvergne) Dip

Ingredients

- 1 (300 g) eggplants, medium size
- 1 cup breadcrumbs
- 2 garlic cloves, crushed
- 1/2 cup fresh parsley, chopped
- 2 teaspoons ground cumin
- 1/2 teaspoon hot paprika
- 2 tablespoons lemon juice
- 1/4 cup yoghurt (natural yoghurt)

Directions:

1. Put the eggplant on tray.
2. Bake at ONE EIGHTY (180) degrees Celsius for approximately ¾ hour or till tender.
3. After this, take out eggplant put in paper bag for TEN min.
4. Take out and remove the eggplant skin.
5. Then chop the flesh.
6. Blend the rest of items with eggplant till become smooth.
7. Refrigerate it.

Pork and Cranberry Sausage Rolls

Ingredients

- 16 ounces ground pork (for Americans) or 500 g pork mince (for Australians)
- 1 cup fresh breadcrumb
- 1/3 cup cranberry sauce
- 1 egg
- 2 tablespoons Worcestershire sauce
- 2 tablespoons sage leaves, chopped
- Sea salt, to taste
- Fresh ground black pepper, to taste
- 3 sheets puff pastry, halved
- 1 egg, extra, lightly beaten
- 2 tablespoons fennel seeds

Directions:

1. Take ground pork, cranberry sauce and mix with bread-crumbs, Worcestershire sauce, salt, pepper and egg in bowl.

2. Put half of mixture into each pastry half and roll it up.

3. Then chop the rolls into pieces.

4. Use the fennel seeds as sprinkle.

5. Finally bake till sausage rolls become golden in color and cooked through

Prawn (Shrimp) Cocktail

Ingredients

- 16 medium prawns, shelled, deveined and cooked
- 1/2 cup low-fat mayonnaise
- 1/4 cup tomato sauce (ketchup)
- 1/4 teaspoon ground black pepper
- 3 drops Tabasco sauce
- 4 small lettuce leaves
- 4 cherry tomatoes, cut into quarters
- 4 teaspoons corn kernels

Directions:

6. Take mayonnaise, tomato sauce and mix them with tomato sauce and pepper in bowl.

7. Blend in a couple drops of Tabasco.

8. Take prawns and add to bowl. And mix well.

9. Put the lettuce leaves in FOUR glasses.

10. Use the prawn mixture for topping.

11. Use the corn kernels and cherry tomatoes as garnishes.

2 Minute Scallops

Ingredients

- 24 good sized scallops
- 1 dash white wine
- 1 tablespoon olive oil
- 1 tablespoon marmalade

Directions:

1. First of all, sear the scallops in heated oil in skillet over moderate temperature setting for ¼ min per side.

2. Take out of skillet.

3. Add in wine.

4. After this, deglaze the pan.

5. Add in marmalade.

6. Swirl all around till sauce become starts to boiling.

7. Then right after this, pour over the scallops.

8. Use herbs as sprinkle.

Asparagus with Garlic Butter and Parmesan Cheese

Ingredients

- 2 bunches asparagus, trimmed of woody ends
- 125 g butter (no substitute)
- 4 garlic cloves, crushed
- Salt and pepper
- 40 g parmesan cheese, grated (finely)

Directions:

1. Heat pan of water to boiling.
2. Then after this, add the asparagus in it.
3. Cook for 120 seconds or till crunchy and soft.
4. Then put in iced water to stop cooking and then drain them.
5. Sauté the garlic in melted butter in skillet over moderate temperature for 60 seconds.
6. Add the salt and pepper.
7. Take asparagus and add to pan, toss well and turning in butter.
8. Distribute into FOUR dishes.
9. Use cheese as sprinkle over each one.

Beer and Scallop Kebabs

Ingredients

- 500 g scallops
- 1 cup beer
- 4 garlic cloves
- 1/4 teaspoon ground black pepper
- 1/4 teaspoon chili flakes
- 1 small onion, chopped
- 8 skewers

Directions:

1. Blend everything together.

2. Keep in refrigerator for 60 min.

3. Put a couple of scallops over every skewer.

4. After this, grill on barbecue over moderate temperature setting for approximately TEN min, turning from time to time.

5. Pour over the preserved marinade.

6. You can serve this delicious recipe with the rest of beer.

Oysters Kilpatrick

Ingredients

- 24 fresh oysters, in their shells
- Rock salt
- 1 tablespoon Worcestershire sauce
- 30 g butter
- 4 slices bacon, rind and all fat removed, finely diced
- Sea salt, to taste
- Fresh ground black pepper, to taste
- 2 tablespoons flat leaf parsley, chopped
- Lemon wedge, to serve

Directions

1. First of all, organize oysters on rock salt bed in shallow dish.

2. Take butter and mix with Worcestershire sauce in saucepan.

3. Heat the butter till melted and mixture starts to get bubbling around the corners of saucepan. Take way from heat.

4. After this, spoon lit bit of butter and Worcestershire sauce over every oyster, use diced bacon for topping each one and add the sea salt and ground black pepper according to your own choice.

5. Cook for FOUR min under grill till bacon become crunchy.

6. Use parsley as sprinkle.

7. You can serve this delicious recipe with lemon wedges.

Mini Corn & Ham Muffins

Ingredients

- 1 cup self-rising flour
- 1 teaspoon baking powder
- 30 g butter, melted
- 1/2 cup milk
- 2 eggs
- 3 slices ham, finely chopped
- 125 g corn kernels, drained
- 2 tablespoons chopped chives
- 1/4 cup cheese, grated
- 1 slice ham, for decorating (optional)

Directions

1. Coat the TWENTY FOUR whole mini muffin pan with cooking oil.

2. Take flour and sift with baking powder in bowl.

3. Tae butter, eggs and mix with milk.

4. Blend this mixture into shifted flour.

5. Add the rest of items besides cheese.

6. Blend well.

7. Take mixture and spoon this into muffin pans.

8. Fill the holes.

9. Use the cheese as sprinkle.

10. Use some of the additional shredded ham as sprinkle as well.

11. Bake till light golden in color.

Australian One Dish Meals

Sausage & Cabbage Casserole

Ingredients

- 1 tablespoon oil
- 8 sausages, pricked
- 60 g butter or 60 g margarine
- 1 onion, thinly sliced
- 1 garlic clove, crushed
- 1 tablespoon tomato paste
- 1/4 cabbage, finely shredded
- 2 Tomatoes, diced
- 2 small zucchini, sliced
- 2 chicken stock cubes
- 2 tablespoons vinegar

- 1 1/2 cups water
- 2 teaspoons brown sugar
- 1/2 cup sultana natural bran
- Salt & pepper
- Topping
- 3/4 cup shredded tasty cheese
- 1/2 cup corn flake crumbs
- 1 slice bacon, diced

Directions

1. Cook the sausages in oil.
2. Take out of pan.
3. Slice and put in casserole dish.
4. Fry the garlic and onion in melted butter till soft.
5. Add in tomato paste.
6. Add in cabbage.
7. Add in tomatoes.
8. Add in zucchini.
9. Cook for a couple of min.
10. Mix the rest of items and heat to boiling.
11. Pour over sausages.
12. Bake, covered, for round about 60 min at ONE EIGHTY (180) degrees Celsius.
13. Mix the topping items and use it as sprinkle.
14. Bake for next TEN min

Risotto with Red Wine and Sausages

Ingredients

- 275 g Italian pork sausages
- 1 tablespoon extra-virgin olive oil
- 2 tablespoons butter
- 1 onion, finely chopped
- 300 g Arborio rice
- 200 ml red wine
- 1 1/3 liters chicken stock, heated
- 2 tablespoons parmesan cheese, freshly grated
- Sea salt
- Fresh ground black pepper

Directions

1. Remove the skin from sausages and pinch meat into skillet. Sauté the meat till golden in color and crusty.

2. Then drain off oil and put the meat aside.

3. Sauté the onion in half of butter and olive oil till tender however not brown in color.

4. Add in rice.

5. Toss well

6. Pour in red wine.

7. Heat to boiling, mixing.

8. After this, add ladle full of hot stock to rice.

9. Blend over moderate temperature till stock is assimilated.

10. Keep on adding stock. This will take approximately 1/3 hour.

11. Add in sausage meat. Blend for next TEN min till rice is cooked however not tender.

12. Turn down heat.

13. Add in parmesan. Add in rest of butter.

14. Add in salt. Add in pepper.

15. Blend through.

16. Allow to rest for a couple of min.

Shepherd's Pie

Ingredients

- 1 ounce butter
- Plain flour
- 1 teaspoon Dijon mustard
- 1 1/2 cups chicken stock
- 2 lbs. lean ground lamb
- 1 tablespoon Worcestershire sauce
- 1 teaspoon dried oregano or 1 teaspoon fresh rosemary, chopped
- Salt
- Pepper
- 3/4 cup milk, hot
- 1 ounce butter, 2 tablespoons
- 4 -6 large potatoes, cooked and mashed

Directions

1. First of all, coat a casserole dish with cooking oil.
2. Fry the onions in melted butter till golden brown in color.
3. Add in garlic and cook for 60 seconds.
4. Take flour, mustard and add them both to pan and mix for 60 seconds.
5. Blend in stock till become smooth.
6. Heat to boiling.
7. Lower the temperature and allow to simmer for THREE min.
8. Add in meat.
9. Add in Worcestershire sauce.
10. Add in oregano.
11. Blend them.
12. Add the seasoning.
13. Take away from heat.
14. After this, spoon this into casserole dish.
15. For preparing potato topping;
16. Mix the rest of items till creamy and smooth.
17. Spread mixture over meat and roll it up.
18. Use the olive oil for coating and bake for ¾ hour.

Sweet Potato and Salmon Quiche

Ingredients

- 250 g sweet potatoes, peeled, cut into 2cm pieces
- Olive oil flavored cooking spray
- 4 green onions, thinly sliced
- 1 garlic clove, crushed
- 2 cups Baby Spinach
- 3 sheets phyla pastry
- 210 g red salmon, drained, skin and bones removed
- 1/2 cup reduced-fat feta cheese, crumbled
- 4 eggs
- 3/4 cup milk
- Dressed salad leaves, to serve

Directions

1. Use the baking paper for lining the baking tray. Put sweet potato in one layer on the tray.

2. Use the oil for spraying.

3. Add the salt and pepper.

4. Roast for approximately 1/3 hour at TWO TWENTY (220) degrees Celsius or till golden in color and soft.

5. Cook the spinach, garlic and onions in oil in skillet over moderate temperature setting for TWO min or till spinach is wilted. Take away from heat

6. Lowe the temperature oven by 40 degrees. Coat one pastry sheet with oil and fold in half. Then put in pan for lining the base as well as sides.

7. Do the same process with the rest of pastry.

8. Take the sweet potato and spoon this over the pastry base. Then after this, spoon over the mixture of spinach.

9. Put salmon in bowl and flake it.

10. Spoon the feta as well as salmon over the mixture of spinach.

11. Take eggs and whisk with milk and salt and pepper in jug.

12. Right after this, pour over filling.

13. Finally, bake the quiche for approximately ¾ hour or till become set.

14. Allow to cool for a couple of min.

15. Slice the quiche

Broccoli, Red Pepper & Tofu Stir Fry With Balsamic

Ingredients

- 14 ounces extra firm tofu, water-packed, drained
- 3 tablespoons balsamic vinegar
- 2 tablespoons reduced sodium soy sauce
- 1 tablespoon honey or 1 tablespoon agave syrup
- 2 garlic cloves, minced
- 1 tablespoon grated ginger
- 1 tablespoon vegetable oil, for broccoli
- 1/2 lb. broccoli floret
- 1 tablespoon vegetable oil, for red pepper
- 1 red pepper, thinly sliced
- 1 tablespoon vegetable oil, for tofu
- 4 scallions, sliced, for garnish

Directions

1. Chop the tofu into SIX slabs.

2. Then chop each of the slab in half for making TWELVE square shapes.

3. Blot the tofu.

4. Take balsamic vinegar, soy sauce and whisk them together with ginger, garlic and honey in bowl and put aside.

5. Fry the broccoli in one tbsp. of oil over moderately high temperature setting till bright green in color and begin to get brown in color in places, approximately FIVE min.

6. Take out broccoli from pan.

7. Fry red pepper in tbsp. of oil over moderately high temperature setting for THREE min or till become brown in color.

8. Take out red pepper from pan.

9. Fry tofu in rest of tbsp. of veggie oil over moderately high temperature setting till brown in color on both of the sides.

10. Take vinegar mixture and add to tofu and allow to simmer till slight thick.

11. Bring the peppers and broccoli back to pan and toss with sauce.

12. Use the scallions as garnish.

13. You can serve this delicious recipe with brown rice.

Bonza Aussie Burger and Chips

Ingredients

- 1 lb. ground beef
- 1 large onion, sliced
- 4 eggs
- 4 slices Canadian bacon
- 4 pineapple rings
- 4 slices cheddar cheese
- 1 (8 1/4 ounce) cans sliced beetroots, drained
- 4 slices Tomatoes
- 4 lettuce leaves
- Ketchup (optional)
- Yellow mustard (optional)

- Dill pickle relish (optional)
- Mayonnaise (optional)
- 4 hamburger buns, split & toasted
- Chips, to serve (French Fries)

Directions

1. Oil the grilling surface.

2. Make four patties from ground beef and grill for FIVE min each side or till cooked through.

3. Sauté the onions in melted butter in sauté pan over moderate temperature setting till tender.

4. Take the onions out of sauté pan and then crack eggs in the same sauté pan over moderate temperature setting.

5. Cook, till yolks become solid, flip over one time.

6. Take out the eggs and put aside.

7. Put the bacon in the same sauté pan and sauté till toasted.

8. Take out bacon and increase the temperature to high.

9. Sauté the pineapple rings in bacon drippings till brown per side.

10. For assembling the sandwiches:

11. Sett the burger bun on a dish and use the burger for topping along with cheese slice and bacon slice and sautéed egg and sautéed onions and a couple of beetroot, tomato slice, lettuce leave and pineapple slice.

12. Put over burger and do the same process again for the rest of burgers.

13. You can serve this delicious recipe with sautéed chips.

Meatlovers Pizza

Ingredients

- 30 cm pizza crusts, with
- Tomato sauce
- 1 cup pizza cheese, grated
- 2 chorizo sausages, sliced
- 125 g cocktail franks, sliced
- 60 -100 g smoked ham, shredded
- 2 tablespoons barbecue sauce

Directions

1. Put the pizza base on sprayed oven tray.
2. Use half of cheese for topping.
3. Then use the sliced meats for topping.
4. Then use the ham and rest of cheese for topping.
5. Bake for approximately ¼ hour at TWO HUNDRED (2oo) degrees Celsius or till top become golden in color and base is crunchy.
6. Take out of oven. And use bbq sauce to drizzle.

Yabbie or Crayfish Fettuccine

Ingredients

- 1 tablespoon olive oil
- 1 onion, finely chopped
- 3/4 lb. sweet potato, diced (400 grams)
- 2 cups water
- 1 (10 1/2 ounce) cans condensed pumpkin soup
- 1 teaspoon curry powder
- Salt and pepper, to taste
- 2 tablespoons cilantro, chopped
- 3/4 cup light coconut cream
- 1 cup milk
- 1 tablespoon corn flour

- 1 lb. fettuccine
- 1 lb. yabbie meat (500 grams) or 1 lb. crawfish meat, poached (500 grams)
- Herbs, sprigs for garnish

Directions

1. Cook the onion in olive oil in pot till translucent however not brown in color.
2. Add in diced sweet potato.
3. Mix over low temperature setting for FOUR min.
4. Add in two cups of water.
5. Allow to simmer for next FOUR min.
6. Add pumpkin soup can.
7. Add in curry powder.
8. Add in seasoning.
9. Add in chopped herbs.
10. Add in coconut cream.
11. Add in cup of milk blended with corn flour.
12. Allow to simmer SIX min.
13. Take away from heat.
14. Heat a saucepan of water to boiling.
15. Add in fettuccine.
16. Boil for TEN min or till ready and done.
17. Drain well and after this, toss with prawns.
18. Use herbs as garnish.

Chicken Cacciatore Risotto

Ingredients

- 3 cups reduced-sodium chicken broth
- 400 g pasta sauce
- 1 tablespoon olive oil
- 100 g pancetta, chopped
- 1 medium brown onion, finely chopped
- 2 garlic cloves, crushed
- 1 1/4 cups Arborio rice
- 1/4 teaspoon dried chili pepper flakes
- 2 teaspoons finely chopped fresh rosemary leaves
- 1/2 cup dry white wine
- 500 g skinless chicken thighs, trimmed, cubed
- 1/3 cup finely grated parmesan cheese
- 1/4 cup roughly chopped fresh flat leaf parsley

Directions

1. Heat the stock and sauce in saucepan to boiling over high temperature.

2. Lower the temperature.

3. Allow to simmer.

4. Sauté the garlic, pancetta and onion in oil in saucepan over moderate temperature, mixing for FIVE min or till onion become tender.

5. Add in rice.

6. Add in chili.

7. Add in rosemary.

8. Cook, mixing for 60 seconds.

9. Add in wine.

10. Heat to boiling.

11. Add in chicken.

12. Mix well.

13. After this, add in ONE THIRD cup of stock mixture.

14. Cook, mixing or till stock mixture is assimilated.

15. Repeat the same process with rest of stock mixture, ONE THIRD cup at a single time, till all of the liquid is assimilated and rice become soft and creamy.

16. Take away from heat.

17. Add the salt and pepper.

18. Use the cheese for topping along with parsley.

Braised Rabbit

Ingredients

- 1 tablespoon olive oil
- 4 (200 g) rabbit, legs seasoned with salt and pepper
- 75 g chorizo sausage, finely diced
- 1 onion, finely diced
- 2 garlic cloves, finely chopped
- 1 large carrot, chopped finely
- 2 sticks celery, finely diced
- 440 g chopped Italian tomatoes, undrained
- 1/2 cup white wine
- 2 cups water
- 1 teaspoon dried thyme

- 3 small potatoes, skin on, quartered
- 1/2 cup frozen peas
- Two tablespoons chopped parsley

Directions

1. Cook the pieces of rabbit in oil in skillet, covered, over high temperature setting, turning till brown in color.
2. Take out to a dish.
3. Add in chorizo.
4. Add in onion.
5. Add in garlic.
6. Add in carrot.
7. Add in celery.
8. Then cook over moderate temperature setting till veggies are cooked through, approximately TEN min.
9. Take thyme, tomatoes, water, and wine and add them to pan.
10. Heat to boiling.
11. Bring the legs back to pan and cover it.
12. Cook for approximately 90 min at low simmer or till rabbit become soft.
13. Take potatoes and add them to pan.
14. Cook for next ½ hour.
15. Blend through peas.
16. Cook for next FIVE min.

Australian Dessert Meals
Christmas Rum Balls

Ingredients

- 10 Vita Brits or 10 Weet-Bix
- 1/2 cup coconut
- 1 cup chopped raisins (optional)
- 2 tablespoons cocoa
- 1 (400 g) cans condensed milk
- 3 tablespoons Bundaberg rum (dark rum)
- Extra coconut or chocolate sprinkles

Directions

1. Blend everything together in bowl.
2. Keep in fridge covered for 30 min.
3. Make balls and after this, roll in coconut.

Cherry and Chocolate Brownies

Ingredients

- 200 g dark cooking chocolate
- 150 g butter, chopped
- 1 cup brown sugar (200g)
- 3 eggs, lightly beaten
- 1 cup plain flour (150g)
- 1 cup desiccated coconut
- 425 g black cherries, pitted, drained

Directions

1. Spray the pan ad line with baking paper.

2. Take chocolate, butter and put them in dish and keep in microwave on moderate power, mixing one time, for TWO min or till butter and chocolate melts.

3. Take sugar and blend into chocolate mixture, mixing well.

4. Blend in eggs.

5. Blend in flour.

6. Blend in coconut.

7. Add in cherries.

8. Take mixture and pour this into pan and bake for approximately ¾ at ONE EIGHTY (18o) degrees Fahrenheit.

9. Allow to cool in pan and then chop into square shapes.

Super Delicious Kiwi Ice

Ingredients

- 2 cups apple juice
- 1 tablespoon lemon juice
- 4 kiwi, peeled and sliced
- 2 tablespoons sugar, Splenda is good too
- 1/2 teaspoon orange rind, grated

Directions

1. Mix the 1ˢᵗ THREE items in food processor till become smooth.

2. Add in sugar. Add in orange peel.

3. After this pulse to mix well.

4. After this, pour into shallow container and freeze for 180 min.

5. Then beat on moderate speed for 120 seconds.

6. Bring back to freeze for next 180 min.

7. Allow to cool for a couple of min.

8. After this, spoon into bowls.

9. Use mint as garnish.

Mini Honey Cheesecakes

Ingredients

- 250 g ricotta cheese
- 1/3 cup caster sugar
- 1/3 cup honey
- 4 eggs
- 1 teaspoon ground cinnamon
- 1 lemon, zest of, finely grated

Directions

1. Take ricotta, honey, sugar and beat them in bowl till become smooth and blended.

2. Add in eggs and beat them well.

3. Mix in cinnamon. Mix in lemon rind.

4. Take mixture and spoon into EIGHT greased muffin pan.

5. Bake for approximately 1/3 hour at ONE EIGHTY (180) degrees Celsius or till become firm.

6. Let cool.

7. Use additional honey to drizzle. Along with berries and dollop of cream.

Easy Eggless Banana Bread

Ingredients

- 4 very ripe bananas, mashed
- 1 1/2 cups all-purpose flour
- 1/2 cup butter, melted
- 3/4 cup brown sugar
- 1/2 cup milk or 1/2 cup buttermilk
- 1 teaspoon baking soda
- 1 teaspoon vanilla essence
- 1 pinch salt

Directions

1. Take mashed bananas and mix with butter.

2. Blend in milk.

3. Blend in milk.

4. Blend in sugar.

5. Blend in baking soda.

6. Blend in salt.

7. Blend in flour till mixed.

8. Take mixture and pour this into bread loaf pan that has been greased and floured.

9. Bake for 60 min or till toothpick comes out neat and clean when inserted in the center.

10. Let cool prior to transferring from pan.

Australian Apricot Loaf

Ingredients

- 1 cup chopped apricot
- 1/2 cup currants
- 1/2 cup sultana
- 1/2 cup sugar
- 1/4 lb. butter, softened
- 2 cups self-rising flour
- 2 large eggs, beaten
- Chopped preserved gingerroot (optional)
- Chopped pecans or walnuts (optional)

Directions

1. First of all, spray the loaf tin.
2. Pour cup of boiling water on fruit, butter as well as sugar.
3. Add in eggs. Then after this, add in flour.
4. After this, you can pour into loaf tin.
5. Bake in medium oven for approximately ¾ hour.

Cappuccino Cupcakes

Ingredients

- 1 teaspoon instant coffee powder
- 1 tablespoon butter, melted
- 1 egg
- 2 tablespoons caster sugar
- 2 tablespoons self-rising flour
- 1/4 cup plain flour
- 40 g good quality dark chocolate, grated
- 1 cup thickened cream
- 1 teaspoon drinking chocolate
- 1 teaspoon cocoa powder
- Cocoa powder, to serve
- Chocolate-covered coffee beans, to serve

Directions

1. First of all, line a patty pan.

2. Take coffee and dissolve in a tbsp. hot water in jug and blend in butter.

3. Beat in sugar and egg in bowl till become pale in color and become thick.

4. After this, sift the flours over mixture of egg.

5. Then fold in till mixed.

6. Blend in coffee mixture

7. Blend in grated chocolate.

8. Use the mixture for filling half of each paper case.

9. Bake for approximately ¼ hour at ONE EIGHTY (18o) degrees or till skewers comes out neat and clean when inserted.

10. Let the cupcakes rest in pan for TEN min and then shift to wire rack for cooling.

11. Beat cream till become thick, after this, sift cocoa and drinking chocolate over cream. And fold it through cream.

12. Take cream mixture and spoon this over cupcakes.

13. Use the additional cocoa for dusting.

14. Use chocolate coated coffee bean for topping every cupcake.

Aussie Style Caramel Slice

Ingredients

Base

- 1 cup self-rising flour
- 1/2 cup brown sugar
- 3/4 cup coconut
- 125 g butter (4oz, melted)

Filling

- 400 g condensed milk
- 1 tablespoon butter
- 2 tablespoons golden syrup

Directions

1. Blend everything together.

2. Press into tray.

3. Bake for ¼ hour at THREE FIFTY (35o) degrees Fahrenheit. Allow to cool.

4. **For filling;** cook all of the items into saucepan over low temperature till butter has been melted and mixed and become golden in color.

5. After this, pour over the biscuit base and bring back to oven for TEN min.

6. Prior to chopping, allow to cool thoroughly.

Apple Fritters with Cinnamon Sugar and Caramel Sauce

Ingredients

Fritters

- Vegetable oil (for deep frying)
- 1/2 cup plain flour
- 1/2 cup self-rising flour
- 2 tablespoons caster sugar
- Cold water (icy cold)
- 2 apples (

Cinnamon Sugar

- 2 tablespoons sugar
- 1 teaspoon cinnamon (ground)

Caramel Sauce

- 60 g butter
- 1/3 cup brown sugar
- 1/2 cup cream (pouring)

Directions

1. For fritters; take oil and pour this into saucepan till full by 1/3

2. Heat over moderately high temperature setting.

3. Take flours, sugar and mix them with enough ice cold water for preparing batter the consistency of thick cream.

4. Take sliced apples and coat them in batter.

5. Then deep sauté for FOUR min or till become golden in color and shift to wire rack for draining.

6. For cinnamon sugar; take cinnamon and mix with sugar in bowl.

7. For caramel sauce, take sugar and mix with butter in saucepan put over moderate temperature and cook for FOUR min or till sugar has been dissolved.

8. Blend in cream.

9. Allow to simmer for THREE min or till sauce become thick.

10. Then put fritters over dishes. Use the cinnamon sugar as sprinkle all over the caramel sauce.

Custard Powder Biscuits

Ingredients

- 125 g butter, softened
- 1 cup caster sugar
- 1 egg, at room temperature
- 1/2 teaspoon vanilla essence
- 1 1/2 cups self-rising flour
- 1/2 cup custard powder
- 80 g white chocolate, roughly chopped

Directions

1. First of all, line the two baking trays.
2. Take butter and mix with sugar till become fluffy.
3. Beat in egg. Beat in vanilla.
4. Take flour and shift with custard powder together over the mixture of butter.
5. Blend in white chocolate till mixture forms a tender dough.
6. After this, take tbsp. of mixture and roll into ball shapes and put them on trays.
7. Then flatten them slightly.
8. Bake till become golden in color.
9. Allow to rest on trays for a couple of min. then shift to wire rack for cooling.

Australian Soups and Stews

Delicious Ham and Potato Soup

Ingredients

- 3 1/2 cups peeled and diced potatoes
- 1/3 cup diced celery
- 1/3 cup finely chopped onion
- 3/4 cup diced cooked ham
- 3 1/4 cups water
- 2 tablespoons chicken bouillon granules
- 1/2 teaspoon salt (to taste)
- 1 teaspoon pepper (white or black to taste)
- 5 tablespoons butter
- 5 tablespoons all-purpose flour
- 2 cups milk

Directions

1. Take the potatoes, celery and mix with water, ham and onion in stock.

2. Heat to boiling.

3. Then cook on moderate temperature setting till potatoes become soft.

4. Blend in chicken bouillon.

5. Blend in salt as well and pepper.

6. Whisk in flour in melted butter in another saucepan. Cook, mixing continuously, till become thick.

7. Blend in milk till all of the milk is added.

8. Keep on mixing over moderately low temperature till become thick.

9. Take milk mixture and blend this into stock pot and cook the soup.

10. Finally, heat through.

Potato, Leek & Ham Soup

Ingredients

- 1 tablespoon olive oil
- 2 leeks, washed and peeled
- 1 kg potato, peeled and chopped
- 1 liter water
- 1 tablespoon vegetable stock powder
- 375 ml evaporated milk, low fat
- 100 g lean ham, sliced
- 1 teaspoon parsley, chopped
- Pepper

Directions

1. Cook the potatoes and leeks in oil in saucepan for 120 seconds.

2. Take mixed veggie stock powder and water AND add to pan and heat to boiling.

3. Lower the temperature and allow to simmer for 1/3 hour.

4. Process the mixture in blender till become smooth.

5. Bring the soup back to pan, and turn heat to boiling.

6. Blend in evaporated milk. Blend in ham.

7. Allow to simmer for 60 seconds.

8. Add the ground black pepper.

9. Blend in parsley.

Aussie Apricot Chicken

Ingredients

- 1 tablespoon oil
- 1 medium onion, sliced
- 1 garlic clove, crushed
- 2 tablespoons flour
- 2 teaspoons curry powder
- 600 g skinless chicken thighs, filets, cut into 3 to 4 pieces
- 1 (40 g) French onion soup mix (dry)
- 1 (415 g) cans apricot nectar
- 2 tablespoons chopped parsley

Directions

1. Saute the garlic and onion in oil in pan over moderate temperature till onion become tender and mix.

2. Take curry powder and mix with flour together in bag and then add to chicken and toss them.

3. Take chicken and add to pan and cook till color is changed.

4. Blend in dry soup mix.

5. Then blend in nectar.

6. Heat to boiling and allow to simmer till mix become thick.

7. Cover and put in oven at ONE NINETY (19o) degrees Celsius for ½ hour or till chicken cook through.

8. Take out of oven and blend through parsley.

Chickpea and Potato Soup

Ingredients

- 2 cups uncooked dried garbanzo beans, soaked for 12 hours, drained
- 2 medium onions, chopped
- 2 medium potatoes, peeled and diced
- salt
- 1/2 teaspoon turmeric
- 1 teaspoon ground cumin
- 1 teaspoon ground coriander
- 1/8 teaspoon cayenne pepper
- fresh ground pepper
- 2 tablespoons lemon juice
- Chopped fresh parsley (to garnish)

Directions

1. Heat chickpeas onions and eight cups water to boiling in pot.

2. Partly cover the pot and lower the temperature and allow to simmer for 60 min.

3. Add in potatoes.

4. Add in salt.

5. Add in spices.

6. Add in next ¾ cup water.

7. Heat back to boiling.

8. Then lower the temperature and allow to simmer for next 90 min on low temperature setting.

9. Blend in lemon juice.

10. Use parsley as sprinkle.

Curried Chicken and Zucchini Soup

Ingredients

- 1 tablespoon low fat margarine
- 1 medium brown onion, chopped finely
- 1 garlic clove, crushed
- 1 teaspoon curry powder
- 1/2 cup basmati rice
- 12 ounces boneless skinless chicken breasts, sliced thinly
- 2 cups water
- 4 cups chicken stock
- 4 medium zucchini, grated coarsely

Directions

1. Fry the garlic and onion in melted margarine in saucepan, mixing till onion become tender.

2. Add in curry powder.

3. Cook, mixing till mixture become fragrant.

4. Add in rice and then add in chicken.

5. Cook, mixing, for 120 seconds.

6. Add in water. Then after this, add in stock.

7. Heat to boiling. And lower the temperature.

8. Allow to simmer for approximately TEN min, covered.

9. Add in zucchini.

10. Cook, mixing, for approximately FIVE min or till chicken cook through.

Smoked Fish Chowder

Ingredients

- 2 large smoked fish fillets (haddock or cod)
- 2 cups potatoes, diced
- 1 cup celery, diced
- 1 large carrot, diced
- 1 onion, diced
- 3 tablespoons butter
- 3 tablespoons flour
- 2 cups milk
- 1 cup tasty cheese
- Mustard (to taste)
- 1 tablespoon Worcestershire sauce

Directions

1. Place all of the vegetables in stock pot.

2. Add water to cover the veggies. Add in tbsp. of stock powder.

3. Allow to simmer till tender.

4. Put two smoked cod over the vegetables and allow to simmer for approximately ¼ hour.

5. Prepare thick white sauce in sauté pan by using THREE tbsp. of butter and flour and TWO cups of milk.

6. Add a tsp of mustard.

7. Add in a tbsp. of Worcestershire sauce.

8. Add in a cup of tasty cheese.

9. Add in black pepper according to your own choice.

10. Blend soup for breaking up fish.

11. Add in cheese sauce.

12. Mix well.

Butter Chicken Soup

Ingredients

- Marinade
- 1 boneless skinless chicken breast, around 200g
- 1 tablespoon lemon juice
- 1 tablespoon ground coriander
- 1 teaspoon cumin
- 1 teaspoon chili powder
- 1 teaspoon grated fresh ginger
- 2 garlic cloves, big ones, crushed
- Soup
- 1 tablespoon butter
- 1 onion, finely chopped

- 1 teaspoon ground coriander
- 1 teaspoon cumin
- 1 teaspoon grated gingerroot
- 1/4 teaspoon chili powder
- 400 g canned tomatoes, diced
- 2 tablespoons tomato paste
- 2 tablespoons plain flour
- 2 teaspoons brown sugar
- 3 cups chicken stock
- 1/4 cup basmati rice
- 1/4 cup light cream
- Natural yogurt and fresh coriander (to garnish)

Directions

13. For preparing Marinade:
14. Finely slice the meat and mix with the rest of items in a bowl.
15. Keep in refrigerator for a minimum of 60 min.
16. For preparing soup;
17. Mix the chopped onion and marinated chicken in melted butter in saucepan.
18. Mix continuously till chicken seals and onion become tender.
19. Add in dried spices.
20. Add in ginger.
21. Blend in tomatoes.

22. Blend in chicken stock.

23. Once simmering, pour in basmati rice.

24. Blend and allow to simmer for TEN min.

25. Take flour and mix it with tomato paste and whisk into soup. Add in cream. Add in brown sugar. And add seasoning according to your own choice.

26. You can serve this delicious recipe in bowls with a dollop of yogurt along with torn up naan bread and coriander.

Lentil Tomato & Chorizo Soup

Ingredients

- 125 g chorizo sausage, thinly sliced
- 1 garlic clove, crushed
- 1 onion, finely chopped
- 400 g brown lentils, undrained
- 400 g diced tomatoes
- 3 cups reduced-sodium vegetable stock
- Chopped fresh parsley (to garnish)
- Turkish bread, for serving

Directions

1. Cook the onion, chorizo sausage and garlic in saucepan for THREE min.

2. Blend in undrained Edgell brown lentils.

3. Add in tomatoes.

4. Add in stock.

5. Heat to boiling.

6. Lower the temperature and allow to simmer, covered, for approximately ¼ hour.

7. Use the parsley as sprinkle.

8. You can serve this delicious recipe with bread.

Roasted Tomato and Red Pepper Soup

Ingredients

- 1 1/2 lbs. red bell peppers
- 2 lbs. Tomatoes, halved and seeded
- 2 tablespoons olive oil
- 1 cup onion, chopped
- 4 garlic cloves, minced
- 1 1/2 cups tomato juice
- 1 tablespoon fresh marjoram, chopped or 1 teaspoon dried marjoram
- 1 1/4 teaspoons black pepper
- 1/2 teaspoon salt
- Marjoram, sprigs (optional)

Directions

1. First of all, vertically chop the peppers and remove the membranes and seeds.

2. Put the tomatoes and peppers on baking sheet that has been lined with foil. Then flatten the peppers.

3. Broil for ¼ hour or till veggies become black.

4. Put the peppers in zip lock bag and seal the bag and allow to rest for TEN min.

5. Chop the peeled peppers and tomatoes.

6. Blend half of the peppers and tomatoes into processor till become smooth and put aside.

7. Fry the onion and garlic for SIX min, mixing from time to time.

8. Raise the temperature.

9. Add in pureed veggies.

10. Add in rest of veggies. Add in tomato juice. Add in chopped marjoram. Add in black pepper. Add in salt.

11. Cook till heated through.

12. Then pour the soup into bowls.

13. Use the marjoram springs as garnish.

Winter Vegetable Soup

Ingredients

- 2 onions, chopped
- 2 stalks celery, sliced
- 2 potatoes, diced
- 2 large carrots or 3 small carrots, peeled and sliced
- 1 large parsnip, peeled and sliced
- 10 ounces butternut squash
- 2 bay leaves
- 1/4 teaspoon thyme
- 1/4 teaspoon marjoram
- 2 cups vegetable stock
- 4 cups water

- 1 cup nonfat yogurt (optional) or 1 cup soy yogurt (optional)
- Ground black pepper
- Soy sauce or salt
- Chopped chives (to garnish) (optional)

Directions

1. Heat all of the veggies, water, bay leaves and stock to boiling.
2. Lower the temperature and allow to simmer till veggies become tender.
3. Let the veggies cool and then puree in blender till become smooth.
4. Bring back to heat and blend in pepper. Blend in soy sauce.
5. Blend in yogurt.
6. Use the chopped chives as sprinkle.

Pie Crust Mushroom Soup

Ingredients

- 400 g field mushrooms
- 1 small onion, diced
- 1 garlic clove
- 1/4 cup plain flour
- 3 cups vegetable stock
- 1 tablespoon thyme leaves
- 1 tablespoon sherry wine
- 1 cup fat-free evaporated milk
- 1 sheet puff pastry
- 1 eggs, beaten or 1 tablespoon nonfat milk

Directions

1. Chop coarsely the peeled mushrooms. Cook the onion in some of liquid in pan till tender.
2. Add in garlic. Cook for 60 seconds.
3. Add in mushrooms.
4. Cook till tender.
5. Use the flour as sprinkle.
6. Blend for 60 seconds.
7. Blend in stock.
8. Add in thyme.
9. Heat to boiling.
10. Lower the temperature to simmer, covered, for TEN min.
11. Let cool.
12. Blend in sherry.
13. Blend in evaporated milk.
14. Then after this, pour the mix into FOUR bowls.
15. Chop the rounds of pastry and cover each of bowl with it.
16. Seal the corners and brush it with egg.
17. Bake till become puffed and golden in color.

Chilled Pear and Chicken Soup

Ingredients

- 825 g sliced pears, in natural pear juice, drained, roughly chopped
- 2 teaspoons light olive oil
- 1 small onion, chopped
- 1 small sweet red pepper, chopped
- 2 stalks celery, chopped
- 1 skinless chicken breasts, diced or 125 g chicken strips, roughly chopped
- 4 cups chicken stock
- 1/4 teaspoon ground cinnamon
- 1/2 teaspoon fresh ginger, grated or 1/4 teaspoon ground ginger
- 2 tablespoons dry white wine
- 4 tablespoons natural low-fat yogurt

Directions

1. Chop the drained pears into chunks and remove the juice and put aside.

2. Cook the chicken, celery, onion and red pepper in oil in skillet over moderate temperature for FOUR min, while mixing.

3. Blend in stock. Heat to boiling.

4. Lower the temperature and keep on cooking, covered, for next TEN min or till red pepper, celery and onion become tender.

5. After this, add in pears.

6. Add in cinnamon.

7. Add in ginger.

8. Add in white wine.

9. Puree the soup in blender till become smooth and shift to the separate bowls.

10. Allow to cool.

11. Put a dollop of yogurt in each of the bowl.

12. Use the sprig of parsley as garnish.

Coriander (Cilantro) Fish Ball Soup

Ingredients

- Broth
- 4 cups fat-free chicken stock
- 2 cm piece fresh ginger, peeled, sliced
- 2 whole star anise
- 4 teaspoons soy sauce
- 2 teaspoons brown sugar
- 1 green chili, divided
- 1 garlic clove
- Balls
- 350 g boneless white fish fillets, skin removed, roughly chopped

- 1/2 cup fresh coriander leaves, chopped
- 1 teaspoon finely grated lime zest
- 1 garlic clove, crushed
- Salt and pepper
- To Finish
- 200 g dried rice-stick noodles
- 1 small head of broccoli, cut into small florets
- 50 g snow peas, trimmed
- 1 bunch asparagus, woody ends removed, cut in half
- Fresh coriander leaves, to serve
- Lime wedge, to serve

Directions

1. Heat the garlic, half of green chili, sugar, soy sauce, stock, ginger and star anise in saucepan to boiling over high temperature setting.
2. Lower the temperature and allow to simmer, covered, for approximately ¼ hour or till reduced slightly.
3. Process the garlic, lemon rind, salt, pepper, coriander and fish in blender till mixed.
4. After this, roll heaped tbsps. of mixture into ball shapes.
5. Put noodles in bowl and add the boiling water to cover the noodles.
6. Allow to rest for SEVEN min or till soft.
7. Drain well.
8. After this, strain stock mixture into bowl.

9. Bring back to pan over moderate temperature.

10. Take fish balls and add to stock mixture. Cook, mixing, for FIVE min.

11. After this, add in broccoli florets through.

12. Cook for 120 seconds.

13. Add in asparagus.

14. Cook for next 60 seconds.

15. Finally, add in snow peas.

16. Cook for 60 seconds or till soft.

17. Distribute the noodles into separate bowls.

18. Ladle the fish balls, veggies and soup over the noodles.

19. Use the coriander as topping.

20. You can serve this delicious recipe with lime wedge.

Bacon and Potato Chowder

Ingredients

- 6 slices bacon, very smokey local bacon is better
- 1 cup onion, chopped
- 1 garlic clove, minced
- 3 cups potatoes, diced
- 3 cups water
- 3 chicken bouillon cubes
- 3 tablespoons flour
- 1 (354 ml) cans evaporated 2% milk

Directions

1. Sauté the bacon till crunchy and chop it.

2. Drain well.

3. Fry the garlic and onion in two tablespoon of bacon drippings in pot.

4. Take potatoes, water, bouillon cubes and add them to pot.

5. Bring to boil and allow to simmer, covered, till potatoes are cooked.

6. Add in bacon.

7. Take flour and mix with small quantity of evaporated milk, form a paste.

8. Blend in rest of milk. After this, add to potato mixture.

9. After this, cook over moderate temperature setting till mixture approaches to boil and become thick.

10. Mix from time to time.

Bestest Hamburger Soup

Ingredients

- 2 lbs. ground beef
- 1/2 teaspoon salt
- 1/4 teaspoon pepper
- 1/4 teaspoon oregano
- 1/4 teaspoon basil
- 1/8 teaspoon seasoning salt
- 1 (2 ounce) packages onion soup mix
- 6 cups boiling water
- 1 (8 ounce) cans tomato sauce
- 1 tablespoon soy sauce
- 1 cup celery, sliced

- 1/4 cup celery leaves
- 1 cup sliced carrot
- 1/3 cup dried split peas
- 1 cup elbow macaroni
- Grated parmesan cheese

Directions

1. Cook the meat in saucepan and then drain extra fat.
2. Add in salt. Add in pepper. Add in oregano. Add in basil. Add in seasoned salt and add in onion soup mix.
3. Blend in boiling water.
4. Blend in tomato sauce. Blend in soy sauce.
5. Allow to simmer, covered, for approximately ¼ hour.
6. Add the carrots, celery leaves and celery to simmering mixture. Add in split peas. Keep on cooking for ½ hour.
7. After this, add in macaroni.
8. Allow to simmer for next ½ hour, mixing often.
9. Use the parmesan cheese as sprinkle over the separate servings.

Australian Salad Meals
Beach Bar Special - Aussie Seafood Salad

Ingredients

- 2 eggs
- 2 tablespoons olive oil
- 3 tablespoons lime juice, about 1 lime
- 2 tablespoons sweet chili sauce
- 2 spring onions
- 1 little gem lettuce
- 198 g sweetcorn with bell peppers, drained
- 140 g cherry tomatoes, halved
- 125 g cooked peeled tiger shrimp

Directions

1. Heat pan of water to boiling.
2. Lower in eggs.
3. Boil for EIGHT min.
4. Then take out and let them cool in cold water bowl.
5. Take olive oil, lime juice and whisk with sweet chili sauce in bowl.
6. Diagonally chop the spring onions into fine slices and blend them into dressing.
7. After this, shell eggs and slice into round shapes.
8. Distribute the lettuce leaves into TWO dishes.
9. After this, top with sweetcorn and scatter the tomato halves all over.
10. Finally, add the prawns and sliced egg and chili dressing over the top.

Brown Rice Salad

Ingredients

- 1 cup brown rice
- 1 3/4 cups water
- 1/4 cup soy sauce
- 1/2 onion, finely chopped
- 1 red capsicum, chopped
- 1/2 cup roasted peanuts, chopped
- 1/2 cup roasted sunflower seeds
- 1/2 cup roasted pumpkin seeds
- 1/2 cup sultana

Dressing

- 1/4 cup olive oil
- 2 tablespoons lemon juice

- 1 teaspoon lemon rind, grated
- 1 garlic clove, crushed
- 1 teaspoon fresh ginger, grated
- 1 teaspoon honey
- Salt, to taste

Directions

1. First of all, cook rice in water and drain well.
2. After this, add soy sauce.
3. Then add chopped onions.
4. Allow to cool.
5. Add in sultanas. Add in capsicum.
6. Add in peanuts and add in seeds.
7. Blend everything together for dressing and pour it over the salad.

Butternut Pumpkin (Squash), Roasted Hazelnut and Feta Salad

Ingredients

- 1 cup hazelnuts
- 1 1/2 kg butternut pumpkin, cut into 3cm pieces
- Olive oil flavored cooking spray
- Salt and pepper
- 175 g marinated Persian feta cheese, drained

Honey and Balsamic Dressing

- 1/4 cup honey
- 2 tablespoons balsamic vinegar
- 1 tablespoon olive oil
- Salt and pepper, to taste

Directions

1. Roast the hazelnuts on baking tray for approximately ¼ hour at FOUR FIFTY (45o) degrees Fahrenheit or till nuts are roasted.

2. After this, wrap in tea towel.

3. Remove the skin by rubbing the hazelnuts in baking tray.

4. Chop these nuts and put them aside.

5. Use the baking paper for lining the roasting pan.

6. Then organize the pumpkin in pan. Use the oil for coating.

7. Then use the salt and pepper for seasoning.

8. **After this, roast, turning one time, for ¼ hour or till soft and become golden brown in color. Allow to cool.**

9. Shake the dressing items in screw top jar. And keep in microwave till honey melts. Shake again.

10. Take feta, and mix with hazelnuts and pumpkin on a dish.

11. Use the dressing for drizzling.

Chicken and Orange Salad

Ingredients

- 2 oranges
- 2 skinless chicken breast fillets, cooked and shredded
- 2 celery ribs, cut into fine strips
- 2 spring onions, shredded
- 1 yellow capsicum, cut into fine strips
- Sea salt & freshly ground black pepper, to taste
- 250 g mixed green salad leaves

Dressing

- 150 ml natural yoghurt or 150 ml Greek yogurt
- 2 tablespoons mayonnaise
- 2 teaspoons honey
- 1 tablespoon fresh parsley, roughly chopped
- 1/2 cup pecans

Directions

1. First of all, peel the oranges in bowl. Chop flesh into segments and put them in bowl.

2. Blend in cooked and shredded chicken.

3. Blend in celery.

4. Blend in spring onions.

5. Blend in capsicum.

6. Add the salt and pepper according to your own choice.

7. **Prepare dressing; blend all of the items in bowl along with preserved orange juice.**

8. **Organize salad leaves and chicken mixture into FOUR dishes.**

9. **After this, pour dressing all over.**

10. **Distribute the pecan nuts into 4 dishes.**

Chicken Coleslaw Pasta Salad

Ingredients

- 150 g spiral pasta
- 3 cups finely shredded green cabbage
- 2 cups skinless cooked chicken
- 1 red capsicum, seeded and thinly sliced
- 1 green capsicum, seeded and thinly sliced
- 1 small red onion, thinly sliced
- 1 carrot, peeled and grated
- 1 celery rib, finely chopped
- 1 small cucumber, peeled and finely diced
- 1/2 cup mayonnaise
- 2 tablespoons coarse grain mustard
- 2 tablespoons red wine vinegar

Directions

1. First of all, cook the pasta as instructed on the package.
2. Drain and rinse.
3. Then shift to bowl and let cool.
4. Take cabbage, chicken, cucumber and add them to pasta along with celery, capsicum onion and carrot and blend well.
5. Take vinegar, seasoning, mustard and mix with mayonnaise, salt and pepper and cabbage.
6. Add to salad. Toss properly well.
7. Allow to chill.

Chicken Salad with Pineapple

Ingredients

- 2 cooked chicken breast halves, chopped
- 1 cup celery, finely chopped
- 2 hard-boiled eggs, chopped
- 2 -3 scallions, finely chopped (green onions)
- 4 -5 canned pineapple rings, finely chopped
- 1 cup good quality mayonnaise
- 1/4 cup mild prepared mustard, to taste (less (or more)
- 1 -2 teaspoon lemon pepper
- Salt and pepper
- 1 tablespoon toasted slivered almonds (optional)

Directions

1. Blend everything together besides almonds.
2. If you salad is very thick, you can add little bit of pineapple juice.
3. Allow to chill.
4. You can serve this exotic recipe over crunchy lettuce.
5. Scatter the almonds all over.

Chicken, Potato and Avocado salad

Ingredients

- 500 g tiny new potatoes, washed well, but not peeled
- 4 chicken thigh fillets
- 4 slices bacon
- 2 tablespoons oil
- 2 Avocados, peeled and sliced
- 2 teaspoons lemon juice
- 2 cups mixed lettuce leaves

DRESSING

- 1/4 cup olive oil (or mix half and half olive and vegetable)
- 2 tablespoons white wine vinegar
- 2 tablespoons chopped fresh herbs
- Salt and pepper

Directions

1. First of all, boil the potatoes for 1/3 hour or till soft.
2. Drain them and allow to cool.
3. Chop the bacon and chicken into strips.
4. Sauté the chicken in oil in pan till cooked.
5. Take out and then sauté the bacon till crunchy.
6. Drain the bacon and chicken.
7. Use the lemon juice as sprinkle all over the avocado.
8. After this, chop the potatoes in halve and toss in dressing with avocado and bacon and chicken.
9. You can serve this exotic and tasty recipe on combined lettuce leaves bed.

Couscous with Zucchini & Tomato

Ingredients

- 200 g baby red capsicums, chargrilled & chopped
- 200 g zucchini, quartered & sliced
- 100 g sun-dried tomatoes, chopped
- 1/4 cup fresh parsley, finely chopped
- 100 g walnuts, chopped
- 200 g couscous
- 4 tablespoons olive oil
- 2 tablespoons lemon juice

Directions

1. First of all, cook the couscous as instructed on package and put in bowl.

2. Blend in three tbsp. of olive oil.

3. Blend in lemon juice.

4. Put aside.

5. Sauté the zucchini in rest of oil till golden in color.

6. Then after this, add to couscous.

7. Sauté walnuts in same pan for 120 seconds, mixing and after this, add to couscous along with the rest of items.

8. Blend well.

Creamy Apple Pecan Salad

Ingredients

- 2 granny smith apples
- 2 golden delicious apples, red
- 2 tablespoons lemon juice
- 1 1/2 cups celery, thinly sliced
- 1/2 cup pecans, roasted & halved

Dressing

- 1/2 cup mayonnaise
- 1/2 cup sour cream
- 2 teaspoons lemon juice
- 1 teaspoon honey
- 1 pinch cinnamon
- 1 pinch nutmeg

Directions

1. Take the apples, core them and quarter them and finely slice them.

2. After this, dip these slices of apple in lemon juice.

3. Mix with celery.

4. Take pecans and add to salad and toss.

5. Use the dressing for topping.

6. For dressing, mix the items.

Kiwi Fruit Salad

Ingredients

- 8 kiwi fruits, sliced
- 2 bananas, peeled and sliced diagonally
- 1 papaya, pared, seeded and sliced

Honey lime dressing

- 2 tablespoons olive oil or 2 tablespoons salad oil
- 1 tablespoon honey
- 1 tablespoon lime juice
- 1/8 teaspoon grated lime zest
- 1/8 teaspoon paprika
- 1 dash salt

Directions

1. Take banana, papaya, and mix with kiwi fruit and toss with honey lime dressing.

2. For preparing honey lime dressing;

3. Mix all of the dressing items. Add salt according to your own choice. And whisk

Marinated Mushrooms

Ingredients

- 250 g button mushrooms, sliced
- 4 tablespoons French dressing
- Fresh ground black pepper
- 1 tablespoon parsley or 1 tablespoon chives, chopped
- Lettuce cup

Directions

1. Take dressing, pepper and mix with parsley and mush-rooms.

2. Toss well.

3. Allow to chill for 120 min.

4. Then drain well and you can serve this delicious recipe in lettuce cups.

Orecchiette with Lentils, Mint and Feta

Ingredients

- 100 g green beans, topped and cut into thirds
- 150 g orecchiette
- 1/4 cup olive oil
- 400 g tinned brown lentils, drained and rinsed
- 2 tablespoons chopped fresh mint
- 1 1/2 tablespoons balsamic vinegar
- 1/2 small Spanish onion, sliced top to bottom very thinly
- 1/3 cup fresh basil leaf, torn
- 100 g feta, crumbled

Directions

1. First of all, heat a large size saucepan of salted water to boiling.
2. Add in beans.
3. Cook for THREE min.
4. Take out the beans and refresh them with water.
5. After this, cook the orecchiette till ready and done.
6. Drain well and put aside.
7. Take lentils, pasta and toss them with herbs and onion and balsamic and oil.
8. Add the salt and pepper.
9. Use the crumbled feta for topping.

Salmon and Potato Salad with Lemon Poppy Seed Dressing

Ingredients

- 750 g chat potatoes
- 100 g snow peas, trimmed and halved
- 100 g smoked salmon, cut into thin strips
- 1/2 yellow pepper, cut into strips
- 2/3 cup plain yogurt
- 1 tablespoon lemon juice
- 1 teaspoon finely grated lemon rind
- 2 teaspoons poppy seeds
- 2 spring onions, finely chopped
- Salt & freshly ground black pepper, to taste

Directions

1. First of all, boil potatoes till soft.

2. Add snow peas to saucepan and cook for 60 seconds.

3. Drain.

4. Let cool.

5. After this, halve potatoes and organize them in bowl with snow peas, capsicum and salmon.

6. Take yogurt, lemon juice and mix with poppy seeds and rind.

7. Add the seasoning according to your own choice and taste.

8. And after this, drizzle over the salad.

9. Use the spring onions as garnish.

Salsa Verde Potato Salad

Ingredients

- 1 kg baby new potato, washed halved, skin on
- 1 cup whole egg mayonnaise
- 1/4 cup chopped dill leaves
- 1/4 cup chopped basil leaves
- 1/4 cup chopped parsley
- 1 lemon, grated rind and juice
- 2 tablespoons baby capers
- 2 tablespoons chopped baby dill pickles
- 1/2 red onion, finely chopped
- 1 garlic clove, crushed

Directions

1. First of all, cook potatoes in saucepan of boiling water for ¼ hour or till soft.

2. Drain them and shift to bowl.

3. Blend the rest of items in bowl and add the seasoning.

4. Take half of mayo mixture and add to potatoes and put aside.

5. Add in rest of mixture and toss well.

Tart and Tangy Potato Salad

Ingredients

- 4 large potatoes, washed and cut into 8 pieces
- 2 tablespoons red onions, finely diced
- 3 hard-boiled eggs, quartered
- 1/4 cup fresh parsley leaves, chopped
- 1 cup light sour cream
- 2 lemons, juice of
- 2 tablespoons olive oil
- 1 tablespoon Dijon mustard

Directions

1. Heat the potatoes in pot of cold and salted water to boiling.
2. Keep on cooking till soft.
3. Drain potatoes and mix with parsley, eggs and onion.
4. Whisk the rest of items and season.
5. Take dressing and pour this over.
6. Let it rest for a minimum of 60 min.

If you enjoy the recipes in this little recipe book, please take the time to share your thoughts and post a review on Amazon. It'd be greatly appreciated!

Thank you and good eating!

Victoria Love
www.AfflatusPublishing.com
www.epicdetox.com
www.secretstoweightlossrevealed.com

Check Out My Other Books

Below you'll find some of my other popular books that are popular on Amazon and Kindle as well. You can visit my author page on Amazon to see other work done by me.

Paleo: The Caveman's Paleo For Beginners: Amazing! The Ultimate Paleo Diet for Beginner's Blueprint for Incredible Caveman's Revenge Paleo Cookbook: 41 Red Hot Melt The Pounds Fast Weight Loss Recipes Uncovered With Your Top Paleo Diet Questions Answered In Never Before Seen Detail

10 Day Green Smoothie Cleansing: The Ultimate Lose 10 Pounds in 10 Days Green Smoothie Detox Blueprint

10 Day Detox Diet: Innovative Diet Plan Transforms Your Life, Instantly Giving You Explosive Energy and Vitality Guaranteed

Vegetarian Slow Cooker Recipes Revealed: Fast Recipes For Slow Delicious Success

Cooking Light in 3 Steps; Cooking Light Has Never Been So Easy; Super-Fast and Light Done Right Cooking Revealed, Simple 3 Step Recipes, Fast Cooking Done Right

Famous Recipes Cookbook; Rediscover 70 All-Time Super Star Classic Recipes

No Wok Takeout: 80 Chinese Cooking Uncovered; 80 Secret, Delicious Ready-In-A-Snap Chinese Cooking Recipes Revealed

You can simply search for these titles on the Amazon website to find them.

Your *Secret FREE Bonus!*

As a preferred client of Afflatus Publishing we strive to provide more value, all the time. As you are now a special part of our family we want to let you in on a little a little secret...

A special thanks goes out to you. So subscribe to our free e-book giveaway. Each week we will spotlight an amazing new title. **Yours absolutely free**.

Click Here to Subscribe For Free Now
https://afflatus.leadpages.net/free-ebook/

Made in the USA
Middletown, DE
11 August 2018